This Book
Belongs to

Betty Miller

A GALAXY OF CLEVELAND'S BLACK STARS 1796–1996

A Bicentennial Activity Book for Children, ages 7–12

New Day Press   **Cleveland, Ohio**

This book is dedicated to the following founding members of New Day Press' Board of Directors who are deceased.

Elizabeth Brown
Frank G. Ceasor, Sr.
Ardelia Dixon
Robert Southgate

Copyright © 1996 by New Day Press

Published in the United States of America
ISBN 0-913678-30-9

Published by:
New Day Press
Karamu House 2355 East 89th Street
Cleveland, Ohio 44106

ACKNOWLEDGMENTS

Editor — Ebraska D. Ceasor

Production Coordinators:
    Charlotte Durant
    Angela Lee

Editorial Committee:
    Martha Smith — Chairman
    Emma Calaway
    Ebraska D. Ceasor
    Edith Gaines
    Shirley Hayes
    Dolores Laney
    Mary Moore

Graphics and Illustrations:
    Charlotte Durant
    Angela Lee

The Ohio Arts Council helped fund this organization with state tax dollars to encourage economic growth, educational excellence and cultural enrichment for all Ohioans.

CONTENTS

Introduction 1

George Peake . . . . *Angela Lee* 2

John Malvin . . . . *Stephanie Grair Ashford* 4

Dan R. Field . . . . *Angela Lee* 6

Joseph Hodge . . . . *Angela Lee* 8

Dr. Latrobe Mottley . . . . *Angela Lee* 9

Dr. Robert Boyd Leach . . . . *Angela Lee* 10

Jane Edna Harris Hunter . . . . *Angela Lee* 11

Justin Miner Holland
Harry L. Freeman
Noble Sissle . . . . *Angela Lee* 13

Langston Hughes . . . . *Stephanie Grair Ashford* 15

Mary B. Martin . . . . *Angela Lee* 16

Zelma Watson George . . . . *Ebraska D. Ceasor* 18

Frederick Grair . . . . *Stephanie Grair Ashford* 20

Jesse Owens . . . . *Marlana Hamer* 22

Douglas Phillips . . . . *Mona Phillips* 24

Ruby Dee . . . . *Stephanie Grair Ashford* 26

Larry Doby . . . . *Stephanie Grair Ashford* 27

Louis and Carl Stokes . . . . *Tyshawn Knight* 28

Madeline Manning Mims . . . . *Stephanie Grair Ashford* 29

Answers 30, 31

Eliza Bryant . . . . *Martha Smith* 34

INTRODUCTION

The New Day Press was incorporated in 1972 and has published twenty-two (22) titles which have been used by many libraries and schools in Ohio and other states. Most of the writers and artists are from Cleveland, Ohio.

This activity book for children is presented to coincide with Cleveland, Ohio's Bicentennial and to spotlight Black Clevelanders who have contributed significantly to Cleveland's growth.

The mission of New Day Press is to give minority-group Americans the opportunity to tell their own stories in their own way. This helps fulfill the charge given by James Weldon Johnson in the Negro National Anthem:

"Facing the rising sun,
Of our new day begun,
Let us march on,
'Til victory is won!"

Current members of The New Day Press Board of Directors

Annie Brabson	Shirley Hayes
Emma Calaway	Dolores Laney
Ebraska D. Ceasor	Angela Lee
Charlotte Durant	Mary Moore
Ruth Emmer	Marsha Pettus
Edith Gaines	Ethel Pye
Hugh Gaines — Emeritus	Martha Smith

Honorary Members of New Day Press

Susanne Hartman Byerley	Michael Luton
Juanita Dalton-Robinson	Ben Shouse

GEORGE PEAKE

1722–1827

George Peake was Cleveland's first permanent Negro settler in 1809. In April with his two sons he crossed the Cuyahoga River near the foot of St. Clair driving his wagon. He became the first wagon traveler on the Cleveland-Rockport Road, now known as Detroit Rd. His journey lead him to a point where he settled now known as Lakewood.

He was a soldier in the British Army. He invented the grist mill which was used for producing meal from grain in a fast and effective way. This invention was highly prized by everyone.

He married a black woman who had a wheel barrow full of silver half-dollars. Together they bought $103\frac{1}{2}$ acres of land which he later willed to his sons. That land was called Ohio City.

George and his family were considered wealthy when he died in Cleveland at the ripe old age of 105.

Activity: Draw George, his wife, and his 2 sons.

Activity: Color this picture of George Peake in his wagon

JOHN MALVIN
1795–1880

John Malvin was born free in Virginia, yet did not learn to read until he was 18 because it was against the law. He decided that he wanted to learn "pretty talking" and found an old slave who secretly taught him to read. In 1827, after becoming a preacher, he walked 300 miles to Ohio because he thought that life would be better there. He made Cleveland his home.

Unfortunately, he found that there were many rules in Ohio, too, that made it hard for African-Americans. The Black Laws did not allow African-American children to attend the public schools. He helped organize the first school for Cleveland's African American children. The school was at a steam mill where Malvin worked, near the mouth of the Cuyahoga River.

When he was a boat captain, he helped runaway slaves to freedom through the Underground Railroad.

Malvin was a charter member of the First Baptist Church. When the church was completed, several members thought that the Black and White members should sit separately, which had been the custom throughout the country. Malvin argued that if Blacks and Whites could go to the same church, the pews should be integrated. After 18 months of discussion, it was decided that all members could sit wherever they wanted.

John Malvin crossed the Ohio River to Marietta, Ohio. From there he worked on a boat along the Ohio River to pay his way to Cincinnati. A few years later, he and his wife took the Ohio River to Portsmouth, traveled by wagon to Chillicothe, and took the Ohio Canal to Cleveland.

Malvin also helped to organize schools for African Americans in Cincinnati, Springfield, and Columbus.

Activity: John Malvin

Find the cities in Ohio where John Malvin helped to organize schools for African-American children. Mark them with a drawing of a school.

DAN R. FIELD

?–1905

Dan R. Field was a former slave. He was one of many blacks who fought bravely in the Civil War. He came to Cleveland, after serving in that war, with his captain. His captain was an architect and they worked together until Dan Field's death in 1905.

On the south side of the Soldiers and Sailors Monument, located on Public Square, is a heroic group in bronze. This monument is in honor of Cleveland men, white and black, who fought in the Civil War. Inside the monument, on the north panel, is relief bronzed art which depicts a group watching President Lincoln lifting shackles from the arm of a slave with his right hand and handing him a musket with his left hand. The slave was represented by Dan R. Field. Dan posed for his own statue! The inscription on the statue reads: ". . . and upon this act, sincerely believed to be an act of justice warranted by the Constitution upon military necessity, invoke the considerate judgment of mankind and the gracious favor of almighty God."

Dan Field was proud to serve his country in the Civil War, a war which gave him the right to be a free man and claim his right to be his own man. This is a privilege we sometimes forget took many lives to achieve.

Activity: Find the monument (hint: center of Public Square) and write your name in the book among the signatures of worldwide visitors. Look for the names of the Civil War Colored troop in the 5th and 27th who sacrificed their lives for the freedom we share today.

Draw a picture of the monument after you find it.

Activity: Color the Civil War combat soldier (jacket, dark blue; pants, light blue) and the Medal of Honor which several blacks were awarded.

JOSEPH HODGE

?

Joseph Hodge led Moses Cleaveland and his party of 48 (45 men, two women, and one child) across the Pennsylvania line to the state of New Connecticut or the Western Reserve. This area was named Cleveland after Moses Cleaveland. Somewhere along the way the "a" was taken out of the spelling of Cleaveland. Joseph's first contact with Cleaveland was in 1796. Moses Cleaveland and his party engaged Hodge, known to them as, "Black Joe." Joseph was chosen for this important task because he was an excellent guide, pilot, and interpreter. Joseph Hodge was needed by Moses Cleaveland because of his familiarity with the land, tricky water of Lake Erie and his knowledge of the Seneca Indians and their language. It is believed that Joseph Hodge had been a runaway slave. Large numbers of black people, like Joseph, were living in New York state at that time. Joseph had a home in Buffalo Creek, New York.

He was married to a native American. One of his sons died fighting for America in the War of 1812. He was also a hunter and trapper. Little is known of Joseph's birth date or his death because during that time records were not well kept but the contributions he made left lasting impressions on the Moses Cleaveland party and on us today.

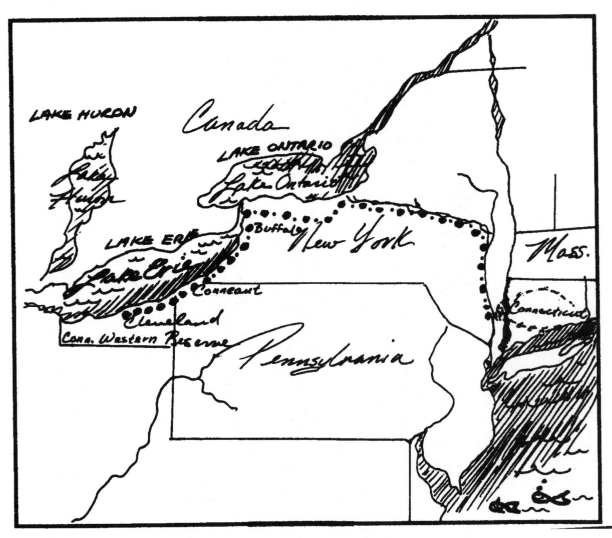

Activity: Connect the dots that show the route that Joseph Hodge led Moses Cleaveland on the expedition to Cleveland, Ohio.

DR. LATROBE MOTTLEY
(?–1914)

Dr. Latrobe Mottley was born in Barbados, British West Indies, exact date unknown. He later came to Cleveland and graduated with honors from Cleveland Homeopatic Medicine College in 1891. He established offices at 51 Huron Rd. while still a senior in Medical school. He was appointed visiting physician. Dr. Mottley was a brilliant medical doctor who established the Cleveland Training School for Colored Nurses in 1898 in his home. The enterprise was incorporated in 1899 and called Bethesda Hospital and Training School for Nurses. He was a well known practicing physician until his death in 1914.

Activity: Color the Cleveland Homeopatic Medicine College.

DR. ROBERT BOYD LEACH

1822–1863

Dr. Robert Boyd Leach was the first black physician in Cleveland, Ohio. He established his practice in Cleveland about three years prior to the start of the Civil War when the black population numbered less than 800. He had both white and black patients. Dr. Leach came to Cleveland in 1844 from southern Ohio without an education. He had a great desire to improve himself and worked on lake steamers. He was given the assignment of nurse for the sick on the boat. He studied medical books in the ship's medicine chest. He read, becoming very familiar with science and medicine. He was credited with compounding a remedy for malaria and cholera which was much in demand around the lakes.

He entered medical school and graduated in 1858 from Cleveland Homeopatic Medical College.

When the Civil War broke out, he helped recruit many Negro soldiers but was refused enlistment because of poor health. Dr. Leach wanted to be a part of the fight to end slavery. He was one of the first to advocate full rights to black citizens. He died of a liver problem at a friend's home on his way to Washington, D.C., in a final attempt to enlist in the war.

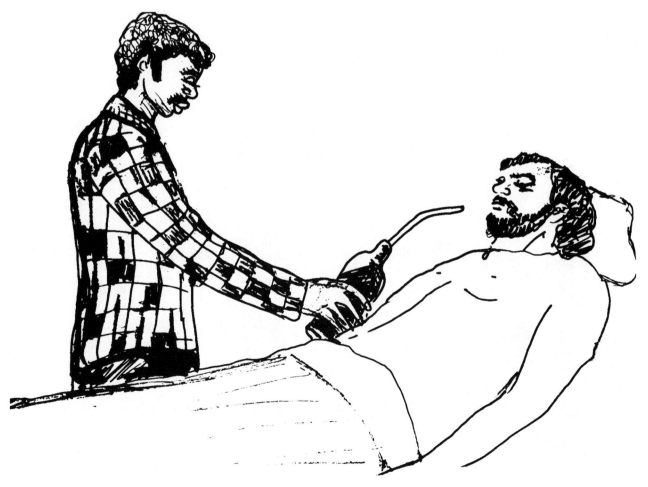

Activity: Color the drawing of Dr. Leach at work.

JANE EDNA HARRIS HUNTER
1882–1971

Jane Edna Harris Hunter was the daughter of a slave and had to support herself as a young teenager. She did this by working as a field hand, cotton picker, and laundress. She managed to educate herself and graduated in 1905 as a trained nurse from Hampton Institute in Virginia. She came to Cleveland that same year after her graduation. She found much prejudice against working women in employment and housing. Her struggles convinced her of the importance of providing decent housing and training for women like herself. She started the Working Girls' Home Association, with dues fixed at one nickel per week, that way anyone could afford to live in decent housing. In 1911 she opened the first home of The Phillis Wheatley Association, a twenty-three room house at Central and East 40th Street. She called it Phillis Wheatley after a Boston slave girl from the 18th century who was considered to have been the first black poet in America.

In six years the need became so great she extended housing to a 75 room building next door. But the need just kept getting greater and greater. There were more sites in 1921 in Glenville, Mt. Pleasant, and on the west side. The need grew and so did her dream. In 1927 she purchased a corner stone at 46th Street and Cedar Avenue and launched a building fund campaign which raised $550,000 and this was matched by a $100,000 grant from John D. Rockefeller, Jr.

This was her dream and the dream building was built from the ground up, nine stories in all. This building would provide the space where the special mission of the Phillis Wheatley Association would be carried out . . . "to discover, protect, cherish, and perpetuate the beauty and power of Negro womanhood."

The Phillis Wheatley Association today, houses women and men. It also houses nine service programs ranging from day care to elderly care and serves residents throughout Cuyahoga County.

She was a remarkable woman who served thirty-seven years as the Association's President, Secretary, and Executive Secretary. She went on to receive a law degree from Baldwin-Wallace College in Berea, Ohio in 1925 and was one of the first women to be inducted into the Ohio Women's Hall of Fame. Recently her name was used for the Cuyahoga County Department of Human Services building at 3955 Euclid Avenue which provides many social services for county residents.

Activity: Color the pictures of Jane Hunter and the Phillis Wheatley Association.

JUSTIN MINER HOLLAND
1819–1887

Justin Miner Holland entered Oberlin College but left at the age of 22, before he graduated. He came to Cleveland to pursue a musical career. He wrote 35 original works and published 300 arrangements. In 1874 he wrote Holland's Comprehensive Method for the Guitar. This book of instructions was considered by critics as the best work of its kind in America and Europe He spoke fluent French, Italian, and Spanish and forged international friendships with the Negro Masons of Ohio and associations with the Grand Lodges of Peru, Portugal, Spain, France, and Germany. He was very active as a leader in the antislavery movement.

HARRY L. FREEMAN
1870–1954

Harry Freeman was a musical genius. During his life he was described by the *Cleveland Press* in 1898 as a "colored Wagner," who was a very famous European composer of the day. He was a noted Cleveland composer-director and violinist. Freeman was 21 years old when he wrote several operas which were produced in Denver and Chicago. In 1901 the Cleveland Symphony Orchestra in concert at Gray's Armory performed parts of his opera "Nada" (now called Zuluki). Mr. Freeman taught music at Wilberforce University in Xenia, Ohio. He left Cleveland in 1912 and went to New York and ran the Freeman School of Music until his death. He was awarded in 1930 for a composer of the first Negro opera produced in New York City.

NOBLE SISSLE
1889–1975

During Noble Sissles' life he became a very famous black composer, band leader, and vocalist. Noble Sissle, who later became a singer of national reputation, came to Cleveland when his father became minister of Cory Methodist Church. In 1914 he and a group of Central High School classmates attempted to enter the Grand Theater and were turned away. He waged a civil suit and won the verdict for himself and his classmates. Noble Sissle established himself in New York's musical circles and toured the vaudeville theaters of the country. He and Eubie Blake received national acclaim. In 1921 their famous musical comedy which featured Josephine Baker became very famous in the United States and over seas. He along with a collaboration with Eubie Blake wrote famous songs "I'm Just Wild about Harry" and "Love Will Find a Way." He had written musicals which were very popular and set the standard for which Broadway musicals would follow.

MUSICAL PUZZLES

How to Play

Step 1: Try to solve the puzzle first by using the letters on the puzzle.
Step 2: Next look at the hint chart to see if you can solve the puzzle.
Step 3: Repeat steps one and two.   Don't stop until you solve it.

Puzzle 1: Title of Song by Noble Sissle

1	2	3	E
4	5	L	6
F	7	8	D
9			
W	10 Y		

Hint:
1: L
3: V
9: A

Puzzle 2: Name three places in the world Justin Miner Holland had friends.

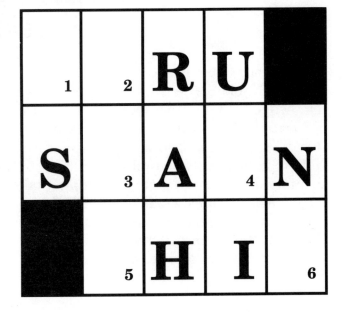

1	2	R	U
S	3 A		4 N
	5 H	I	6

LANGSTON HUGHES

1902–1967

Langston Hughes was born in Missouri, but started writing poetry when he attended Central High School in Cleveland, Ohio. Though he moved away from Cleveland when he graduated, he returned many times. He wrote many plays that were performed at Karamu House.

Langston became the most famous writer in Harlem, New York in the 1920's. He remained popular as a poet, novelist, short story writer, and playwright until his death.

Activities:

Fill in the blanks to complete
this poem by Langston Hughes.

DREAMS

Hold fast to _____

For if dreams die

Life is a broken-winged _____

That cannot _____.

_____ fast to dreams

For when _____ go

_____ is a barren field

Frozen with _____

What are your dreams?
Draw pictures or write words to
describe the dreams you are holding.

15

MARY B. MARTIN

1877–1939

Mary B. Martin was the first Negro elected to the Cleveland Board of Education in 1930. She was brought to Cleveland in 1886 by her parents. After completing her education she taught in Birmingham, Alabama and Cotton Plant, Arkansas. Once her children were grown she longed to return to Cleveland and did. She taught in several schools in Cleveland prior to her election to the Cleveland Board of Education.

She was put into office and kept there by votes from all sections of the City. She had served two successive four year terms but declined the nomination in 1937. The same committee induced her to seek office in 1939. She won a third term but died before she could take office on November 19, 1939. Mrs. Martin's death was considered a great loss and her campaign for intelligent and fair education was a loss the entire community, black and white, would miss. She also has a school named in her honor, Mary B. Martin Middle School, located at 8200 Brookline Ave.

Activity: Draw a picture of MBM School.

Activity: Color Mary B. Martin at her school desk.

ZELMA WATSON GEORGE

1903–1994

Zelma George became a Clevelander in 1942, when she received a grant from the Rockefeller Foundation to study Black music and wanted to research Cleveland Library's John G. White Collection famous for its material on African-Americans.

Zelma's marriage to Attorney Clayborne George, in 1944, kept her in Cleveland, except when she was studying and traveling. She completed work on her doctorate degree in Sociology-InterCultural Relations at New York University in 1954 and took a six month lecture tour around the world on a grant from the United States Department of State in 1959. She was appointed by President Eisenhower in 1960 to the United States Delegation of the 15th General Assembly of the Nations. She received honorary doctorate degrees from Cleveland State University and Baldwin-Wallace and Heidelberg Colleges. She won "Alumnus of the Year Awards" from New York University and the University of Chicago, where she did her undergraduate work. She served as a judge in the Miss America contest in 1969.

Zelma George was also an opera singer. She sang the title role in the *Medium* at Karamu Theatre in Cleveland and on Broadway in New York City. She was outstanding in Menotti's *The Consul* at Cleveland's Playhouse and sang in Karamu's production of *The Three Penny Opera*.

She served as the Director of Cleveland's Job Corps Center from 1966 to 1970.

Mrs. George was born in Hearn, Texas in 1903 and died in Cleveland, Ohio in 1994.

ZELMA GEORGE CROSSWORD PUZZLE

ACROSS

1 Zelma's husband
6 Recognition for hard work
8 Company of actors
9 Everyone
11 Come ashore
12 The Play _____
14 Zelma _____ many awards
15 Had dinner
17 "_____ it now"
20 Not true
21 Not any
22 Job _____
24 Make a loan
26 Zelma was the _____ at Karamu Theatre
28 Zelma won "The _____ of the Year Award"
30 Zelma was the Medium at _____ Theatre
32 Zelma received a Doctorate from _____ University (2 words)
33 The source of light

DOWN

1 Zelma was married in _____
2 Clayborne was an _____
3 Zelma was _____ in Hearn, Tex.
4 Zelma received a grant from the _____ Foundation
5 President _____ appointed Zelma to the General Assembly of Nations
7 Zelma was a _____ to the General Assembly of Nations
10 United States of America (abbr.)
13 Depart
16 Spinning toy
18 Zelma was an _____ singer
19 Connecting word
23 Total
25 Question
27 Opposite of down
29 "It's the _____"
31 Me and you

18

ZELMA GEORGE CROSSWORD PUZZLE

FREDERICK DOUGLAS GRAIR SR.
1913–1987

When Fred Grair was brought to Ohio as a young boy he said he would never return to Alabama. He kept that promise by making Cleveland his permanent home.

Fred was always a hard worker. Along with other part-time jobs, he sold his mother's pies on street corners while he was in high school. In the late 1930's Fred and his friends formed the Twelve Counts Social Club. They bought a building at E. 96th and Cedar to provide a place for Negroes to go. Fred was the club president for several years. The group was known for its elegant balls, fashion shows, and fund-raisers.

In 1946 Fred became the first Negro salesman in the country for Kirby Vacuum Cleaner Company. By 1948 he had broken the world's record for selling Kirbys. In 1954, "Mr. Kirby" opened his own shop which became a training center for young Negroes who wanted to learn to become salesmen.

Like the famous speaker, Frederick Douglass, Fred was a gifted speaker. Throughout his lifetime, he gave speeches at church functions, social gatherings and business meetings.

Unscramble the words to find Fred Grair's favorite motto.

ew okwn otn het dwor ilfa

__ ____ ___ ___ ____ ____

Activity: Draw a vacuum cleaner.

Activity: Color Fred brown
Color his suit and hat black
Choose a color for his tie

JAMES CLEVELAND "JESSE" OWENS
1913–1980

Jesse Owens is remembered today as one of the greatest athletes in sports history. On September 12, 1913, he was born James Cleveland Owens in Orville, Alabama. His parents, Henry and Emma Owens, were poor sharecroppers. In search of a better life, the Owens family relocated to Cleveland in the early 1920's. Soon after, James Cleveland Owens became known as "Jesse."

Although thin and sickly as a child, Jesse eventually excelled as a runner. Early in his athletic career, he broke world records, even as a student at East Technical High School and later at Ohio State University.

His greatest athletic achievements were at the 1936 Summer Olympic Games held in Berlin, Germany. There, he won a record four gold medals in track and field events. After winning his first for the 100-meter race in 10.3 seconds, he was pronounced "the World's Fastest Human." His performance at these games also disproved Adolph Hitler's belief that black people are inferior.

Jesse Owens' athletic feats made him a legend. However, he is still recognized for other outstanding accomplishments, especially his work as a goodwill ambassador. In 1973, he received the Presidential Medal of Freedom from President Gerald R. Ford. Ten years after his death from lung cancer (March 31, 1980 in Tucson, Arizona), Mrs. Minnie Ruth Solomon Owens, his widow, accepted the high honor, the Congressional Gold Medal from President George Bush.

Numerous awards, scholarships, and track meets still bear the Jesse Owens name. There is a Jesse Owens Museum at Ohio State University. Even the street leading to the Berlin Olympic Stadium is now known as "Jesse Owens Strasse."

Activity - Math Olympics

Math Table
12 inches = 1 foot

3 feet = 1 yard = 36 inches

5,280 feet = 1 mile = 1,760 yards

1 inch = 2.5400 centimeters

1 foot = .3048 meters

1 yard = .9144 meters

1 mile = 1.6093 kilometers

Activity - Jesse Owens

1. In school, Jesse Owens was famous for running the 100-yard dash. How many feet is 100 yards? Since 3 feet equals 1 yard, multiply 3 times 100 to get the correct answer.

2. At 15, Jesse Owens could run 100 yards in 11 seconds. Divide 11 into 100 to find out how many yards per second Jesse was able to run. Round your answer to the nearest hundreth of a decimal.

3. At the State Interscholastic Finals, held on May 20, 1933, Jesse Owens broke the world record for high school students in the broad (long) jump. His distance was 24 feet and $3\frac{1}{6}$ inches. Multiply 12 times 24 and add it to $3\frac{1}{6}$ inches to find out the total inches he jumped.

4. At the 1936 Berlin Olympics, Jesse ran the 100-meter race, not the 100-yard race he typically ran in America. To find out the difference in distance between the two races, multiply 100 (which represents the yards) by .9144 (1 yard = .9144 meters) to find out how many meters equal 100 yards. Round your answer to the nearest hundredth of a decimal.

5. Jesse Owens received his first gold medal for running the 100-meter finals in 10.3 seconds. Divide 10.3 into 100 to find out how many meters per second Jesse ran. Round your answer to the nearest hundredth of a decimal.

6. His second gold medal was for setting a new Olympic record for the broad (long) jump, 26 feet $5\frac{5}{16}$ inches. Multiply 12 times 26 and add it to $5\frac{5}{16}$ inches to find out the total inches he jumped.

WORK SHEET

DOUGLAS PHILLIPS
1922–1995

Douglas Phillips was born in Farrell, Pennsylvania. He started drawing pictures of imaginary people and inventing stories about them when he was a young lad. His family moved to Cleveland when he was seventeen.

During World War II, he served as a sergeant in the Army Quartermaster Corps in New Guinea, Australia, the Phillipines, and Japan. He attended the Cleveland Institute of Art and later earned a degree in Fine Arts at Syracuse University.

Douglas got a job as designer with a firm that made church furnishings, including stained glass windows. He was so excited to see his drawings turn into brilliant glass that he decided to specialize. He opened Phillips Stained Glass Studio, Inc. in 1952.

He became famous for his marvelous sense of design and his skill in portraying people. His windows can be seen in churches all across America and in England.

Churches in the Cleveland area where samples of Mr. Phillips' work can be seen are: Mt. Sinai Baptist, 7510 Woodland Avenue; Triedstone Baptist, 3782 Community College Avenue; St. James AME, 8401 Cedar Avenue; St. Gregory Byzantine Catholic, 2035 Quail Street; and Sts. Peter and Paul Roman Catholic, 4759 Turney Road.

Douglas has exhibited at the Women's City Club, The Cleveland Playhouse, The Intown Club, and the General Electric display at Nela Park during the Christmas season.

He coached young fencers at Cleveland State University for many years and taught martial arts classes.

He died August 24, 1995 at his vacation home in Bemidji, Minnesota. His stained glass studio is still in operation, producing windows in the style he created.

Activity: Color "St. Martin De Porres"—A black saint

USE BRIGHT COLORS

RUBY DEE
1923–

Although Ruby Ann Wallace was born in Cleveland, Ohio, her family moved to Harlem when she was still a baby. Her mother, a teacher, insisted that the children study literature and music. The family spent evenings reading poetry.

Ruby decided to become an actress while attending Hunter High School in New York City. She started acting in the 1940's and studied acting with Sidney Poitier and Ossie Davis, whom she later married, at Harlem's American Negro Theater.

Ruby has had acting parts on stage, television, and in movies. She was the first African-American actress to play major parts at the American Shakespeare Festival and has appeared in some of Spike Lee's movies. She and her husband hosted a television series in 1981. Ruby is also a writer, storyteller, and poet.

Currently, Ruby Dee and Ossie Davis host the African Heritage Network's "Movie of the Month" Series, which is the first and only feature film package that focuses on movies showcasing African-American actors, producers, and directors since movie-making began. The African Heritage Network airs in ninety-two (92) markets across the country.

Activity: Ruby Dee retells the Liberian Folk Tale, *Two Ways to Count to Ten*. In the story, the king of the jungle, the leopard, is looking for the cleverest animal to marry his daughter and rule the kingdom after he dies. He has a contest for all the animals in the jungle. The winner must throw his hunting spear into the air and count to ten before it hits the ground. Many animals try, but the antelope wins the contest. Fill in the blanks to find out how the antelope wins the contest.

1   2   3   4   5   6   7   8   9   10

___   ___   ___   ___   ___

LARRY DOBY
1923–

Lawrence Eugene Doby was the first African-American to play baseball for the American League. Born in Camden, South Carolina, Larry lived with relatives for the first fourteen years of his life. After graduating from eighth grade, he moved to Patterson, New Jersey to be with his mother. At Eastdale High School, he received eleven varsity letters in baseball, basketball, and track. He also played baseball and basketball with teams outside the school. Doby played basketball in college, served in the Navy during World War II, and played baseball in the Negro League.

On July 3, 1947, Larry Doby became the first African-American ballplayer on an American League team, the Cleveland Indians. Doby was a left-handed hitter who started as a second baseman with the Tribe. The next season, he got a starting position as a center fielder and became a star. In 1948, Doby played in 121 games, had 132 hits, 14 home runs, and 66 runs batted in. He led the American League in home runs in 1952 and 1954 (32 home runs) and had five seasons with over 100 runs batted in. The Indians went on to the World Series twice when Doby was on the team (1948 and 1954). He played in the All-Star games from 1949–1954.

Even though he was a very talented ball player, he still had to deal with a prejudiced society. Doby could not room with his teammates nor did he travel with the team on a regular basis until the 1954 season because he was an African-American.

Doby was traded to the Chicago White Sox at the end of the 1955 season, but he returned to Cleveland as a coach in 1974.

Activity: Answer the following questions

1. Larry Doby was the first African-American to play _____ in the American League.

2. What sports did Doby play in high school?

3. What position was Doby playing for the Cleveland Indians when he became a star?

4. Doby started traveling and rooming with his teammates on a regular basis in what year?

5. Doby returned to the Cleveland Indians in 1974 as a _____.

27

LOUIS AND CARL STOKES
1925–   1927–1996

The Stokes brothers, Louis and Carl, were born and educated in Cleveland, Ohio. Both brothers earned law degrees from the Cleveland Marshall Law School; Louis in 1953 and Carl in 1956.

Louis Stokes is currently a member of the United States House of Representatives, where he has served with distinction since 1968. He chaired the Select Committee on Assassinations and the House Ethics Committee, and was a member of the Iran-Contra Investigation Committee. Louis was also the co-founder of the Congressional Black Caucus.

In 1967, Carl B. Stokes was elected mayor of Cleveland, becoming the first African-American to serve as mayor of a major United States city. He was anchorman for WNBC-TV in New York City. He returned to Cleveland and served as a judge in the Municipal Court from 1983 until 1994, when he was appointed by President Bill Clinton as United States Ambassador to the Republic of Seychelles, an island nation off the coast of Africa. Carl died on April 3, 1996 in Cleveland, Ohio. He had come home because of illness.

Activity: Louis and Carl Stokes: Unscramble the underlined words to complete the sentences.

1. Louis and Carl Stokes were born in <u>lvecadeln</u>.

2. Louis and Carl both received <u>wla sgrdee</u>.

3. Louis is a member of the United States <u>soeHu</u> of Representatives.

4. Louis was <u>udfeoncro</u> of the Congressional Black Caucus.

5. Louis was <u>nhraiCam</u> of the Select Committee on Assassinations and the House Ethics Committee.

6. Carl Stokes was the first African-American to be elected <u>royam</u> of a major United States city.

7. Carl was an <u>acnohmarn</u> of WNBC-TV.

8. Carl served as a <u>dujge</u> in the Cleveland Municipal Court.

9. <u>rPsedinet</u> Clinton appointed Carl <u>Admasobars</u> of the Seychelles Island.

10. Carl died <u>iprAl</u> 3, 1996.

MADELINE MANNING MIMS
1948–

Madeline Manning Mims, born and raised in Cleveland, first became interested in track and field events through the Cleveland Recreation Division. She attended John Hay High School, and later received a full athletic scholarship to Tennessee State University. She became the first World Class American woman in the 880 yard/800 meter run. While a student at Tennessee State, she set a world record of 2:18.4 in 1967. She also set an American record of 2:02.3 when she won the 800 meter at the Pan-American Games.

Despite her achievements, Madeline had one wish — to represent Uncle Sam (United States) in the Olympics. Her wish came true. She qualified and ran in the Olympics three times. Madeline won a gold medal in the 800 meter at the 1968 Olympics in Mexico City. Her time was 2:00.9. In 1972, she won a silver medal in the Olympics for the 4x400 meter relay.

After retiring from the Olympics, she began competing again in 1975 and became the first American woman to break two minutes in the 800 meter. During her career, Madeline was the national indoor and outdoor champion in the 800 meter several times.

Madeline Manning Mims was named to the All-Time, All-Star Indoor Track and Field in 1983, and is a member of the U. S. Track and Field Hall of Fame, the National Track and Field Hall of Fame, and the Olympics Track and Field Hall of Fame.

Activity: Find the hidden words, which can read forward, backward, up, down, and diagonally.

Champion	All Star
Track	Gold Medal
Field	Silver Medal
Hall of Fame	Meter
Olympics	Scholarship
John Hay	Mexico City
Cleveland	Tennessee
Relay	Event
Uncle Sam	Record
Athlete	

B	U	T	E	N	N	E	S	S	E	E	N	P	T
I	D	G	B	C	R	V	O	A	H	G	J	R	I
C	G	A	D	O	B	E	K	Y	F	E	I	T	F
M	O	C	L	H	U	N	C	L	E	S	A	M	S
E	L	P	E	X	J	T	Y	A	H	N	H	O	J
T	D	S	I	L	V	E	R	M	E	D	A	L	C
E	M	A	F	F	O	L	L	A	H	X	P	Y	L
R	E	C	O	R	D	A	R	H	C	Y	D	M	E
V	D	E	Y	D	M	G	M	L	A	K	X	P	V
K	A	T	H	L	E	T	E	L	J	O	N	I	E
A	L	L	S	T	A	R	E	S	N	M	K	C	L
D	V	P	I	H	S	R	A	L	O	H	C	S	A
F	U	M	E	X	I	C	O	C	I	T	Y	L	N
Q	E	L	N	O	I	P	M	A	H	C	L	N	D

29

ANSWERS

Page 5 — John Malvin

Schools at:
1 Cleveland
2. Columbus
3 Springfield
4 Cincinnati

Page 15 — Langston Hughes

1. dreams
2. bird
3 fly
4. Hold

5. dreams
6 Life
7 snow

Page 14 — Noble Sissle
Puzzle 1

1. L
2. O
3. V
4. W
5. I

6. L
7. I
8. N
9. A
10. A

Page 14 — Justin Holland
Puzzle 2

1. P
2. E
3. P

4. I
5. O
6. O

Page 20 — Fred Grair

We know not the word fail

Page 19 — Zelma George Crossword Puzzle

Page 23 — Jesse Owens

1. $3 \times 100 = 300$ feet
2. 100 divided by $11 = 9.09$ yards per second
3. $12 \times 24 = 288 + 3\frac{1}{6} = 291\frac{1}{6}$ inches
4. $100 \times .9144 = 91.44$ meters, so 100 meters is a longer distance than 100 yards
5. 100 divided by $10.3 = 9.71$ meters per second
6. $12 \times 26 = 312 + 5\frac{5}{16} = 317\frac{5}{16}$ inches

Page 26 — Ruby Dee

<u>2</u> <u>4</u> <u>6</u> <u>8</u> <u>10</u>

Page 27 — Larry Doby

1. baseball
2. baseball, basketball
3. center field
4. 1954
5. coach

Page 29 — Madeline Manning Mims

B	U	T	E	N	N	E	S	S	E	E	N	P	T
I	D	G	B	C	R	V	O	A	H	G	J	R	I
C	G	A	D	O	B	E	K	Y	F	E	I	T	F
M	O	C	L	H	U	N	C	L	E	S	A	M	S
E	L	P	E	X	J	T	Y	A	H	N	H	O	J
T	D	S	I	L	V	E	R	M	E	D	A	L	C
E	M	A	F	F	O	L	L	A	H	X	P	Y	L
R	E	C	O	R	D	A	R	H	C	Y	D	M	E
V	D	E	Y	D	M	G	M	L	A	K	X	P	V
K	A	T	H	L	E	T	E	L	J	O	N	I	E
A	L	L	S	T	A	R	E	S	N	M	K	C	L
D	V	P	I	H	S	R	A	L	O	H	C	S	A
F	U	M	E	X	I	C	O	C	I	T	Y	L	N
Q	E	L	N	O	I	P	M	A	H	C	L	N	D

Page 28 — Louis and Carl Stokes

1. Cleveland
2. law degrees
3. House
4. co-founder
5. Chairman
6. mayor
7. anchorman
8. judge
9. President, Ambassador
10. April

31

Activity: Draw a picture of your own Black Star

Activity: Draw a picture of your own Black Star

ELIZA SIMMONS BRYANT
1827–1907

Eliza Simmons Bryant grew up on land owned by her family in Wayne County, North Carolina. This was very unusual because she was an African-American. She was born 38 years before the Civil War, which ended black slavery in the United States. This family, however was free. Early records show that they owned property and were counted in the census. Slaves were not allowed either of these rights.

Eliza's mother was Polly Simmons. In 1858, Eliza, along with her mother and brothers, John and Buckner, left their North Carolina home for Cleveland, Ohio. There, she married and raised a family.

In 1893, when Eliza was 66 years old, she asked members of Black churches to donate money to buy a house where Black people, who had no family, could live and be cared for. Even though Cleveland was in the free state of Ohio, there were no homes for aged Black people. Within three years, she raised funds and the institution, "The Cleveland Home for Aged Colored People" was opened in 1896. The address was 284 Giddings Avenue. Now, in 1996, it is both a nursing home and a Senior Center and bears the name of its founder, Eliza Simmons Bryant. This beautiful building is located at 7201 Wade Park Avenue.